TATTOO ┊ TATÚ

For Finbar
mo ghrá

Tofu Love, Love Tofu
– Vegan Graffiti, Cork

Nuala Ní Chonchúir

Tattoo ⋮ Tatú

ARLEN
HOUSE

Published in 2007 by
ARLEN HOUSE
an imprint of Arlen Publications Ltd
PO Box 222
Galway
Phone/Fax: 353 86 8207617
Email: arlenhouse@gmail.com

Distributed in North America by
SYRACUSE UNIVERSITY PRESS
621 Skytop Road, Suite 110
Syracuse, NY 13244–5290
Phone: 315–443–5534/Fax: 315–443–5545
Email: supress@syr.edu

ISBN 978–1–903631–60–7, hardback
(a signed and numbered limited edition is also available)

Typesetting ¦ Arlen House
Printing ¦ Betaprint

Cover art work is by Marcus Hughes, Anne Arundel
College, Baltimore, Maryland. See his website at
www.urban-graffiti.net

Tugann Bord na Leabhar Gaeilge
tacaíocht airgid do Arlen House

Bord na
Leabhar
Gaeilge

Contents | Clár

Thit mé i ngrá leis an nGaeilge agus mé i mo chailín óg ag freastal ar an mbunscoil i mBaile Átha Cliath. Agus, díreach mar a bhíonn le gach leannán, bím féin agus an teanga thuas seal agus thíos seal. Uaireanta bím go hiomlán i ngrá leis an nGaeilge, uaireanta eile bím cantalach léi.

My love for the Irish language began as a four-year-old girl in Scoil Mhuire in Marlborough Street in Dublin. It was an all-Irish school, our classes were tiny and I was lucky because I loved learning and our teachers were enthusiastic. The basis I got there carried me through enjoyable stints in the Gaeltacht in An Fál Carrach in Donegal and in An Fheothanach in Kerry; right though a degree in Early and Modern Irish in Trinity College, Dublin and a Masters in Irish Language Translation in Dublin City University. Irish was the language of the classroom, as well as of my social life – sometimes even of my love life – during those years, while English was the language of my home.

Chaith mé mo chuid ama ar scoil agus, níos déanaí, ag an tríú leibhéal, ag labhairt Gaeilge. Sa bhaile, cé go raibh Gaeilge réasúnta ag gach éinne sa teach, níor labhramar ach Béarla. Nuair a thosaigh m'athair ag labhairt Gaeilge linn, dúramar leis éirí as. Tuigtear dom anois gur ghnáthrud a bhí ansin – tharla an rud céanna ina lán teaghlach ina raibh na páistí ag freastal ar Ghaelscoileanna. Ach thaitin sé go mór liom nuair a chasadh m'athair na hamhráin a d'fhoghlaim mé ar scoil: *Báidín Fheidhlimidh, Óró 'Sé do Bheatha 'Bhaile, Táimse im Chodladh,* agus a leithéid. Bhí cumhacht ársa ar leith ag baint leis na hamhráin sin nár aithin mé in aon amhrán sa Bhéarla.

In the mid-nineties I decided to move west. In Galway city, I worked in an Irish language organisation for a year, translating and promoting the language among the business community. I sent my son to Scoil Iognáid, an all-Irish school, and attended the odd Irish medium event. But, after a while, Irish no longer was a central part of my life. Ironically, it was after a number of years in Galway that I began to ease myself away from the language and its supporters. In the place I'd thought would be a sort of mecca for Irish, I found language snobbery that I hadn't encountered in Dublin: relative fluency wasn't sufficient anymore; it appeared the way I pronounced my words wasn't good enough.

I began to dedicate myself more seriously to writing and most of what emerged – prose and poetry – was in English, with just the odd poem in Irish. My passion for literary translation – first discovered in college – remained, and I worked on translating other people's poetry from Irish, most enjoyably Caitlín Maude's stark, unnerving work. But I retained a sort of wariness of some of the members of the Irish language 'movement' I had encountered and, mentally, began to tar all Gaeilgeoirí with the same brush.

Luckily, however, I attended a workshop run by two wonderful Irish language women poets; suddenly I found people who were supportive and honest and open about the status and beauty of Irish, but who understood both my reservations about some of its 'supporters' and my love for the language. That was a turning point in my perception of Galway and Irish. I let the language sneak back and found my heart opening to it again.

Bhí an t-ádh liom gur bhuail mé leis an mbeirt úd. Thuig mé go raibh mórghrá agam don teanga, ach níor thuig mé mo dheacrachtaí léi, ná le lucht na Gaeilge. Cheap mé go raibh mé liom féin. Tar éis labhairt leis na banfhilí, bhí tuiscint níos fearr agam ar an neamhfhoirfeacht a bhain le mo chuid Gaeilge féin. Thuig mé freisin go raibh stór saibhir agam agus go raibh cead agam mo Ghaeilge a úsáid, cé nach raibh sí beacht go hiomlán.

Individual responsibility is spoken of in many contexts these days and, as far as Irish is concerned, I know that if I'm not willing to speak the language, support it and enjoy it, I've only got myself to blame if my connection with it suffers. My Irish is not word-perfect and neither do I put on an accent when I speak it, but I try my best to speak it well. I agree that the language should be spoken as correctly as possible, but those that are making a good fist of it need encouragement, not criticism. TG4, I feel, has been a God-send to Irish in many ways; it has pulled the language into the realm of the young and the modern which, in order to survive, is where it needs to be. County and City Councils can ensure the preservation of place-names in Irish, by giving them parity of esteem on signage and in texts of all descriptions: a visible language has a chance at being a living language.

Irish language writing has long been daring and provocative, unafraid of the realities of human behaviour and interactions, in all their ugliness, beauty, honesty and dishonesty. It can only help, I feel, to bring more translated work to those who don't speak the language – in tandem with the source text –

so that while the reader can enjoy the meaning, she can also compare it to the original in Irish. These poems in *Tattoo : Tatú* are what I would call 'versions' of each other. It is impossible to literally translate a poem and still find a poem in the translation with sense and meaning intact. So I have transposed these poems into English (or Irish) as a version of the original, and hopefully, in the process, have come up with a new poem.

There is a concision and beauty to Irish that I don't find in English: it's a clever, ornate and pretty language that I'm privileged to have in my personal store of knowledge. I'm grateful to my parents for gifting it to me through their choice of schools for me as a child. I have to say that I still resent some of the posturing that is carried on in the name of Irish language preservation (e.g. elitism, exclusion etc.). But there are those who are nurturing of the language and its speakers, and who are open to the changes and evolvements that any language must allow. And they are the ones, I'm sure, who will carry Irish safely through the years ahead.

Mo bhuíochas duit as an leabhar seo a thógáil i do lámha. Tá súil agam go léifidh tú na dánta agus go mbainfidh tú sult astu, cibé teanga ina léann tú iad.

Nuala Ní Chonchúir
Béal Átha na Sluaighe, Bealtaine 2007

TATTOO | TATÚ

TATTOO

My body is a palimpsest
under your hands,
a papyrus scroll
unfurled beneath you,
waiting for your mark.
I clean my skin,
scrape it back to
a pale parchment,
so that your touch
can sink as deep
as the tattooist's ink,
and leave its tracery
over the erased lines
of other men.

You are all that's
written on my body.

TATÚ

Is pailmseist mo chorp
faoi do lámha,
paipír ársa
scrollaithe fút,
ag tnúth le do rian.
Glanaim mo chraiceann,
sciúraim siar é
go pár báiteach
ionas go bpúchfaidh
do lámh mar
dhúch tatuála,
ag líníocht thar
línte dofheicthe
gach fir eile.

Níl faic ach tusa
scrábáilte ar mo chorp.

SEX

An older boy
his front to my back
hooked around me

His brother nearby
leaping in the shadow
of a glasshouse

Their mother blows
long on a whistle
the signal for home

He unpins me
both laugh in my face
I wobble, free

o

You lap through
the cleated velvet
at my core

Burrowing your tongue
along milky lines
and I blossom

My arcing back
and kneading fingers
are your welcome

When you unpin me
we laugh together
I wobble, free

GNÉAS

Déagóir, a chliabh
le mo dhroim
é croctha orm

Tá a dheartháir
ag léimnigh faoi
scáth tí gloine

Séideann a máthair
ar fheadóg – tá sé
in am dul abhaile

Scaoileann sé mé
deineann siad gáire,
tá mé faoi chrith, soar

o

Bolgann tú
an veilbhit fhillte
atá ceartlár ionam

Ag tochailt do theanga
trí línte lachtacha
go mbláthaím

Is fáilte iad mo
dhroim lúbtha agus
mo mhéara a fhuineann

Nuair a scaoileann tú mé
deineann muid gáire, is
tá mé faoi chrith, saor

BODY HAIKU

Folded between my
thighs, an oyster, with edges
that quiver, frill, pulse

Lying between your
legs, an orchid, that blossoms,
blooms on the stalk, wilts

Haiku Coirp

Fillte idir mo
leasracha, oisre, ag crith
is ag frithbhualadh

Ina luí idir
do chosa, magairlín, ag
leathnú, díbholgadh

Oh

you shake me out
in our bed that smells
of sea-salt and *cava*
I cover my belly
offer you my back
an unpuckered
body part

your mouth
suckles, pulls,
scooping out
of my fig-flesh
a long, ancient cry
the unseated whoosh
that shakes, rattles, settles

Ó

croitheann tú amach mé
inár leaba atá salach le
salann agus seaimpéin
clúdaím mo bholg
tugaim mo dhroim duit
craiceann nach
bhfuil craptha

Diúlann do liopaí,
súnn agus slogann,
ag sluaisteáil as
m'fheoilfhige
scairt fhada, ársa
an húis allta a chritheann,
a ritheann, a mhaolaíonn

MY THIGHS ARE COLD

My thighs are cold.

As is the pucked sag of my belly,
a cool appendage hanging like
a symbiotic twin from my waist,
with two sons-worth of skin stretch.

My fingers are cold.

As are my toes, their ten plus ten
equalling twenty long digits
that grapple at warmth with
a cadaver's marblous grip.

Until my morning bed.

There, heat oozes like piety
to every cranny, making
a smug bitch of me, a pup
languishing in self-made heat.

Tá mo cheathrúna fuar.

Is tá mo bholg fuar freisin,
ag luascadh cosúil le
duine breise ó mo chom,
é leathan ó mheáchan mo mhic.

Tá mo mhéara fuar.

Is mo mhéara coise freisin,
fiche lúidín fada,
ag cuardach teasa
le greim an mharbháin.

Go dtí leaba na maidine.

Ansin, leathann teas tríom
cosúil le naofacht,
ag déanamh bitseach díom,
ag sínteoireacht i mo theas féin.

PINK LUNGS

When they clatter past,
all gothic-eyed
and hippy-dressed,
with skin as pure
as a plaster Virgin,
you watch them cup fag ends,
suck on them like inhalers,
and all you can think is
'Your lungs, your lungs,
your pretty pink lungs',
and you know it'll
take them a decade,
or longer, to even begin
to think about it.

SCAMHÓGA ÁILLE

Ritheann siad tharam,
dúshúileach,
fadsciortach,
le craiceann chomh mín
le dealbh den Mhaighdean.
Tá siad ag sú ar thoitíní
cosúil le leanbh ar líreacán,
is ritheann sé liom:
'Bhur scamhóga,
bhur scamhóga,
bhur scamhóga áille'.
Ach tuigim go dtógfaidh sé
deich mbliana nó níos mó orthu
aon mhachnamh a dhéanamh.

GHOST

Our ghost has a
high, pissy smell,
he smokes fags
in the bathroom,
lingers when
I'm feeling low,
throws a shawl
of ice around me,
he watches us
making love,
delights in my lust.
After, he lights up,
belts his flasher's coat,
retreats to the attic.
Our ghost likes me,
but not my lover.
He'll settle soon.

TAIBHSE

Tá boladh fuail
ónár dtaibhse,
caitheann sé toitíní
sa seomra folctha,
fanann sé i mo theannta
nuair atá lagar spride orm,
cuireann sé fuarfháilte
romham i ngach seomra,
faireann sé orainn
ag déanamh suirí agus
is aoibhinn leis mo dhrúis.
Nuair atáimid sásta,
lasann sé toitín,
téann sé suas san áiléar.
Taitníonn mise
lenár dtaibhse,
ní thaitníonn mo leannán.
Rachaidh sé i gcion air.

HARRY KERNOFF REPLIES TO AN ACCUSER

Prolific is not quite
the right
word

Creative might be
a better
one

LABHRANN HARRY KERNOFF AMACH

Torthúil?
Níl sé
sin beacht.

Cruthaitheach –
sea,
sin é é.

STANDING MALE NUDE

If the sculptor
had you recline,
supine like a woman,
all your hummocks and
hollows smoothed out,
made horizontal,
would you be unmanned?

FEAR NOCHT INA LUÍ

Má dúirt an dealbhóir leat,
'Luigh siar, droim faoi,
le gach cnapán agus
logán cothrom',
dromchla mín déanta díot,
an mbeadh tú
dífhearaithe?

FRIDA KAHLO'S PALETTE

Crimson
is prickly-pear blood
it's the most lively

Coffee brown
is *mole*, dying leaves,
dry earth.

Yellow,
it's craziness – my fear –
part of the sun, joy.

Cobalt blue
fizzes electricity,
it's purity and love.

Leaf green:
new leaves, sadness,
the whole of Germany.

Greenish yellow:
the underclothes of all ghosts
reek of it.

Dark green
is the colour of bad advertising
and good business.

Navy blue:
distance, the night sky,
and tenderness.

SPADALÁN FRIDA KAHLO

Corcairdhearg:
fuil an phiorra dheilgnigh
an dath is beoga

Caifedhonn
mole, duilleoga feoite,
cré thirim.

Buí, dath gealtach
– tá faitíos orm roimhe –
an ghrian, gliondar.

Cóbalt
gorm leictreach,
fíor-rud, grá.

Glas na nduilleog:
leathanaigh nua,
An Ghearmáin uilig.

Buíghlas:
tá na fobhrístí ar thaibhsí
bréan leis.

Buidéalghlas:
'sé dath mífhógraíochta
agus dea-ghnó é.

Dúghorm:
achar fada, spéir na hoíche,
agus cineáltacht.

Black:
nothing is
really black, nothing.

Red,
is it only blood?
Ah, who knows?

Dubh:
níl rud ar bith
fíordhubh, rud ar bith.

Dearg,
an fuil amháin é?
Bhuel, an bhfuil a fhios ag éinne?

QUARRY MEN, DUBLIN, 1868

In the heart of the quarry
where stone hides stone
they unearthed a cist;
inside it, a squat burial box
rattling with white bone:

a skull part, a lower jaw,
a fragment of finger,
one tooth fang, a toe,
a slice of rib, a thighbone,
a scatter of oyster shells.

To pass the time
– they were only bones –
they tossed them to each other,
broke them all to shards.

Sa Chairéal, Baile Átha Cliath, 1868

I gcroí an chairéil
áit a bhfuil cloch ar chloch,
aimsíodh uaigh;
istigh ann, bhí cónraín
ag cleatráil le cnámha:

cuid de bhlaosc,
corrán géill, méar,
fiacail, méar coise,
slisín easna, cnámh leise,
sliogáin oisre.

Mar chaitheamh aimsire
– ní raibh iontu ach cnámha –
chaith na fir lena chéile iad,
bhris siad ar fad iad.

Virgin Birth, From Finish to Start

I lie cold
in a laneway
forty stab wounds

pulled from needles
a half-knitted blanket
'Cover it' a voice says

the grasp of rough fingers
I squeak, gulp at air
mother drops

a girlish cry,
they shout at her
I am pulled

push on and on through
walls of wet warmth
heading forward

I am womb-slung
growing under
a school uniform

mother lies,
between her legs
pain and heat

a brother leaves
her bedroom
again

Breith Mhaighdeanúil, Ó Dheireadh go Tús

Tá mé fuar
i mo luí i lána
daichead poll ionam

stróicthe ó bhioráin
pluid leathdhéanta
'Clúdaigh é', deir guth

greim atá garbh
ligim béic
tosaíonn mo mháthair

ag gol go híseal
scréachann siad
tá mé sractha uaithi

brúigh, síos agus síos
trí theas agus taise
brúigh ar aghaidh

i gcoim mo mháthar
ag fás go ciúin
faoina culaith scoile

mo mháthair ina luí,
pian agus teocht
idir a leasracha

fágann deartháir
a seomra
arís

LINGO

Don't know the lingo,
always moaning and groaning
and stressing me out.

You say that you're lost,
that your folks are all brown bread;
don't believe a word.

Get in a round there
and knock back that pint, will ya?
Céad míle fáilte.

BÉARLAGAIR

Níl an *lingo* agat,
is tá tú do mo thachtadh
le do shíorgheonaíl.

Deir tú, 'Ní thuigim',
is go bhfuil do mhuintir marbh;
ní chreidim focal.

Ardaigh do ghloine
agus caith siar an piont' sin.
Céad míle fáilte.

ENGAGEMENT, 1933

He gave me spuds:
lumpers and croppers,
big ones and small ones,
hard and soft ones.

He gave me poteen
it burnt my throat,
but made lying with him
that little bit easier.

He gave me his children:
a half-reared pair,
they were shy, obedient,
the babes of his first love.

He gave me my own child,
it grew under my apron,
before I left my father's,
I was innocent, pliable.

He gave me spuds,
as white as the moon,
as yellow as turnip,
they were bitter, poisonous.

All he gave me
was a dog's life.

CLEAMHNAS, 1933

Thug sé dom prátaí:
cnapáin agus póiríní,
iad mór agus beag,
iad crua agus bog.

Thug sé dom poitín
a las tine i mo ghoile,
ach a rinne an luí leis
ábhairín níos éascaí.

Thug sé leis clann:
péire leathfhásta,
iad cúthalach, béasach,
páistí a chéad ghrá.

Thug sé leis báibín,
a d'fhás faoi m'aprún,
sular fhág mé m'athair,
mé soineanta, solúbtha.

Thug sé dom prátaí,
chomh bán leis an ngealach,
chomh buí le tornapa,
iad searbh agus nimhneach.

Níor thug sé dom
ach meas madra.

PURPLING

What is there
now that you're gone,
but:

shadow-fronted buildings
under a cold morning sky,
the memory of veins
tightening under your skin,
twilight on grey-wet slates
covering the roof-ribs,
lilac branches that bring
bad luck through the door,
an ink-well, dark with
unintelligible lines,
the Advent candle
counting down to Christmas.

What is there,
but the colour of our mourning
for you?

CORCRACHT
i gcuimhne ar Nessa

Céard tá ann nuair
nach bhfuil tú ann ach:

scáthaghaidh na bhfoirgneamh
faoi spéir fhuar na maidine,
camsholas ar cheann slinne
ag clúdach easnacha an tí,
d'fhéitheacha teann faoi
chraiceann do lámh,
an chraobh liathchorcra
ag tarraingt mí-ádh sa teach isteach,
tobar dúigh as a dtagann
línte doimhne, dothuigthe,
coinneal na hAidbhinte
ag comhaireamh i dtreo na Nollag.

Céard tá ann ach
dath ár gcaointe duitse?

NESSA AS FRIDA

Even in death
my sister looked
like Frida Kahlo,
her puckered chins
a mirror of the artist's
on *her* deathbed.

Her crow-black hair
was gone, of course,
but her face still held
features that were Frida's:

Beetle eye-brows,
pretty bow lips,
oriental curved eyes,
killer cheekbones.

And all that
snowy satin and gauze,
the flash of the
red bandanna,
made her coffin festive,
Kahlo-style.

NESSA INA FRIDA

Fiú agus í básaithe
bhí mo dheirfiúr
cosúil le Frida Kahlo,
a smig craptha
faoi mar a bhí smig
Frida ar leaba a báis.

Bhí a gruaig dhubh
imithe, dar ndóigh,
ach fós bhí Frida
le sonrú inti:

Malaí leathana,
liopaí dea-dhéanta,
súile an Oirthir,
géarchnámha gruacha.

Agus rinne
an sról sneachtach
agus deirge
a *bandanna*
rud féiltiúil, Fridaúil
as a cónra.

ENCLOSED

Within this skin
please find enclosed:

a mind
over-giddy
with endless worry

a soul
wispish as mist
alien to its owner

a heart
self-broken and
bruised like fruit.

If you intend
to open it

be prepared:
it *will* bleed.

INIATA

Iniata leis
an gcraiceann seo tá

meabhair
atá meadhránach
le himní

anam atá
chomh neamhshaolta,
dothuigthe le ceo

croí atá
féinbhriste,
brúite mar úll.

Má tá sé ar intinn agat
é a oscailt

bí ullamh:
doirtfear fuil.

THE THIRTEENTH DISCIPLE

I'm no Mary Magdalen.

I won't wet your feet with my tears,
and my hair won't dry your toes,
and you can be sure, there's no hidden jar
of precious spikenard,
to anoint you with when needed.

But, what I have I'll share with you:
my ears to listen, my eyes to guide,
my share to nourish you and slake your thirst,
my arms to protect, the balsam of my body.

And though I won't stand at the bottom of your cross,
or cry and lament at an empty tomb,
I can promise you all of my strength, and,
an ally as constant as a thirteenth disciple.

AN TRÍÚ DEISCEABAL DÉAG

Ní haon Mháire Mhaigdiléana mise.

Ní bheidh do chosa deoirfhliuch toisc sileadh mo shúl,
ná ní ghlanfaidh folt mo chinnse do lúidíní coise,
agus bí cinnte de nach bhfuil próca lán le spíocnard
   luachmhar
curtha i bhfolach agam le coisreacan a chur ort nuair is
   gá.

Ach, pé méid atá agam, roinnfidh mé leat é:
mo chluasa le héisteacht, mo shúile mar threoir,
mo chuid mar chothú, mo lacht mar dheoch,
mo bhaclainn mar chosaint, mo chorp mar bhalsam.

Agus cé nach mbeidh mé ag seasamh ag bun croise
ná ag gol is dod chaoineadh ag tuama atá folamh,
geallaim duit anois go mbeidh mé daingean agus dílis,
díreach mar a bhí i gcónaí an tríú deisceabal déag.

A Kind of Forgery

I take your verse,
slit it with my pen
to see what's hidden
in its deep inside,
then I flip it over,
to winnow out
the secrets that
cower underneath.

Your thoughts
I transmogrify,
stripping them back
to a primitive form,
then I cloak them
in another lexicon,
hanging a new flesh
on older bones.

Each phrase matters
if not each word.

FALSAÍOCHT

Tógaim do dhán,
scoiltim le mo pheann é,
chun an méid
atá ceilte
a thochailt amach,
iompaím bun os cionn é
chun breathnú ar a bhfuil
i bhfolach faoina bhun.

Claochlaím
do smaointe,
tá siad anois
nochta, bunúsaithe,
ceilim faoi
fhoclóir nua iad,
craiceann úr ar
sheanchnámha.

Tá gach frása trom
mura bhfuil gach focal.

YARN

Let me be
your Ariadne,
my fingers fixed
to one end
of an untwining
ball of yarn
that your hands hold.

I will guide you
through the labyrinth,
tunnels, all of your
dark places,
pulling you safe
towards me
and the light.

SNÁTH

Is mise
d'Ariadne,
lig dom,
le mo mhéara,
an snáth
i do lámh
a scaoileadh.

Treoirfidh mé
thú, trí do
chathair ghríobháin,
trí na tolláin,
gach áit dhorcha,
is beidh tú slán liomsa
faoin tsolas.

AND THEN
after Gerry Murphy

And then, of course,
your down-soft hair
your eyes of Liffey and moss
your ears of shell and curlicue
your nose of slope and steam
your mouth of sizzle and fizz
your lips of pucker and pull
your tongue of brass and honey
your voice of breakneck forgiveness
toppling down the wires to soothe me

your throat of dip and tenderness
your shoulders of silk and steel
your back of strength and curve
your arms of tattoo and sanctuary
your hands of languor and urgency
your chest of power and perfection
your belly of pleasure and plenty
your *bod* of bellowing nectar
waiting to be caught

your buttocks of drumlin and valley
your thighs of secretive splendour
your calves of ox and sinew
your feet of oh-so-welcome spontaneity
all of you.

Seaglass will not break:
it's a slice of the bottle
flung to the waves,
cradled around a hopeful note;
or a shard of lantern slipped
from a storm-tossed deck.

Each fragment wears
its personal patina:
scour-smoothed, translucent,
sedge-green, seagull pale.
They finger the dull piece,
linger over it with their eyes.

'You fit more easily into my life,
than I into yours', she says.
His reply?
'Seaglass will not break'.

SAINT PATRICK'S DAY, GALWAY

Two tame-as-a-lapdog elephants
march their own private parade
across Quincentennial Bridge,
their keepers suited and smiling.

> I buy a moonstone, to balance
> my raging yin and yang, try to
> sidestep splats of piss and vomit,
> the gaggles of green-clad drunks.

A footpath slaps up to meet me,
my sober steps none too careful,
kneecaps and pride dented, I joke
ruefully with the ambulance crew.

DUBLINIA

You are pocked
with snot-green rooftops
the crenulated riff
topping Liberty Hall
the loftiest of them all

You are pricked
by the Spire
that lords it over
a push-me-pull-you
of buses, taxis, cars

The Liffey swills
right through you
rushing on to
empty her bladder
on the Muglin Rocks

and your suburbs sing
'Joyrideride, joyrideride'.

The mill race wore an algae cloak, and cowpats littered our path in the hard-mud field. Elderberries popped between filthy fingers left bruisy stains. We took minnows and tadpoles in jars from their Liffey home and left them to live and die in a yellowing sink in the yard, while we rushed off, in wellies and homemade trousers, ready for the next adventure. We built huts in bushes, had secret meetings and scoffed Curly-wurlies until the air got cold and it was time to go in. The hush-hush of the weir was our lullaby.

o

Nine windmills chop the air, swooping their sails above Derrybrien. The mud ankling them heaves downwards, rents the flank of Slieve Aughty. Nine windmills summon a clatter of brothers. They hover above the lake, watching the heron who waits to bill-stab his prey. A heavy-winged launch glides him over bull-rushes, trailing like a mist to the bank, where his motionless stance begins again. This is how to pass a day.

Rain-Cloud, N6, Craughwell, Galway
after Campbell McGrath

Now an anvil-shaped cloud is cow-eye blue and silver,
falling grey and water sodden, celestial green and
Atlantic aqua, Connemara mountain light, Maamturk
blue, John Deere and wheely-bin blue, true, blue of the
heavy heart, blue of mist-hovering tarmac, Motorway
sign blue, the blue of headstones leaning in a tidy
graveyard, skin and eye blue, bruise and corpse blue,
blue anvil morphing to a mushroom cloud with a flat
plateau, spreading to spill its load over already
sopping Craughwell, over the blue of Our Lady of
Knock, blue of the Virgin of hares, Virgin of elections,
Virgin of petrol and oak tree, Virgin of motorist and
school-teacher, Virgin of artist and mother, Virgin of
loneliness, Virgin of rain.

THROUGH THE DEEP
for Séamus Hosey

Like an island fisherman,
the tarred hump of the *currach*
lying light under his legs,
you never learnt to swim,
said the sea couldn't be trusted.

Now you wash and sway
like an unwieldy flotsam,
losing your way through
the fish-shoals, bladderwrack
and hordes of glutinous jellyfish.

The plunge and suck of the sea
heavier than a blue whale
pressing down on your bones,
pulls you through fathoms,
each one the distance between
a fingertip and a fingertip
on your outstretched arms.

Virginia's Last Walk

The day collapsed on me:
there was nowhere to go
but full forward,
so my feet stepped on,
surer than I that
there was no way back.

I loaded the pockets
of my smock with
stone on grey stone,
and stood on the bank
smelling the river-stink,
watching the churn of weeds.

A wood-pigeon broke
from a high branch,
and I lifted my head
to the slap-flutter of wings,
the flash of a purple throat –
a momentary distraction.

I eased myself into the Ouse,
let its wet fingers mangle me,
and the weight of my dress
pull me down and down.
The river swallowed me,
closed in over my head.

The day had collapsed:
I had nowhere to go
but full, fast forward,
so my feet stepped on,
surer than I that
there was no way back.

Like Dogs to War

*'As soon as war is declared it will be impossible to hold
the poets back. Rhyme is still the most effective drum'*
                                    – Jean Giraudoux

A snakeline of soldiers breaks the 6am hush
of the departure lounge at Shannon airport,
their faded combats marking them out.

I stare at their faces, war-wary, young,
shorn girls and boys on their way to a fight,
their sergeant says 'Is this a great country, or what?'

Their nametags read like a map of the world:
Hernandez, Bacus, Berg, Lewis, Savati, Lim,
Casillas, Pitsinger, Bull, Morales, Gray, Velazquez.

The till flaps with the weight of their greenbacks,
traded in for chocolate, pints, triangular sandwiches,
they line up at the phones to tell Mom they're fine.

A drunken Irishman says 'We're proud to have you
      here',
before he slieveens off, badmouthing them as he goes.
I wonder will their names make it onto a monument.

Their nametags read like a map of the world:
Hernandez, Bacus, Berg, Lewis, Savati, Lim,
Casillas, Pitsinger, Bull, Morales, Gray, Velazquez.

BONJOUR, MONSIEUR GAUGUIN

He stands, gruff as fuck,
at my gate, a cloth cap
raked over one eye,
the cape-shouldered coat
making a brown bear of him,
his wooden-clogged feet
both out-turned, ballerina style.

'Bonjour, Monsieur Gauguin',
I say, eyeing his yappy dog.
'Madame', he says, 'my hangover
doesn't allow me to smile, but
the blue-bouldered sky and
ochre fields I've painted you into
are my way of saying "Bonjour"'.

NUDE

She is the Mona Lisa
with breasts exposed,
a chub-faced girl wearing
a woman's worn knuckles

She is the third Grace
daring to hook the gaze
of every hard-won
onlooker

She is the Rokeby Venus
her perfect back a
distraction from her face –
a blur in the mirror

She is Phyllis
her long arms clasped
around the chest of
her moon-pale lover

She is Ingres' *Nude Woman*
cradling her body
against the darkness
that might smother her

She is Psyche
curving her eyes and hips
away from Cupid and his
reposing penis

DOMESTIC GODDESS, CATCHING THE BUS
after Edith Vonnegut's painting

Her face as diffident as Persephone, she flies,
white breasted and exuberantly nippled,
over chestnut trees, turloughs and vetch.

In one hand, a flame-orange scarf, in the other,
her *putto*-son, his stubby penis dangling,
and a plastic lunchbox secure in his fist.

We are not whirling without purpose,
she thinks, *we have buses to catch.*

OUR LADY OF DUBLIN

I am the black Madonna
– Our Lady of Dublin by another name –
I have no swinging *paidrín,*
even this crown is not my own;
my downcast eyes and oak-dark robes
bear no marks from my colourful past.

To save my skin, my paint was stripped:
I was un-whited, de-blued, turned black,
my back was torched, hollowed out with an awl,
then filled with swill for the snuffling swine.

I lolled for a time in a pawnbroker's window,
watching all life unfurl along clattery Capel Street;
I crossed the soupy Liffey then – left the Northside
for the loftier South – in the arms of a priest.

Now I stand, in relief, against alabaster marble,
with a scatter of man-saints: Valentine, Albert, Jude;
Jesus leaps in my arms and the golden crown
they topped me with is shameless with jewels.

I am the black Madonna
– Our Lady of Dublin by another name –
I have no swinging *paidrín,*
even this crown is not my own;
my downcast eyes and oak-dark robes
bear no marks from my colourful past.

La Pucelle

In the hush of my father's house,
before dusk rustles over the horizon,
I take off the dress my mother made
– it's as ruby-red as St. Michael's cloak –
and with a slitch of linen, bind my breasts.

By the greasy light of a candle,
I shear my hair to the style of a boy,
in the looking-glass, I see my girlhood
swallowed up in a tunic and pants,
I lace them tightly to safeguard myself.

My soldiers call me '*pucelle*', maiden,
they cleave a suit of armour to my body,
and know, when following my banner
over ramparts into Orléans, that
there will only ever be one like me.

When the pyre-flames fly up my legs,
I do not think of the Dauphin,
or my trial as a heretical pretender,
but see my mother, head bent low,
sewing a red dress for her daughter to wear.

"MAGGIE M.", GALWAY GAOL, 1892

Before her release, Maggie asked for ten shillings
to buy fruit to sell

I send two letters to them at home and get back none
The Magistrate says I'm a prostitute of the lowest type
Windfalls hawked from a basket make a living for one

The pilfering of a pocketwatch has me inside again
The Governor takes no pity on us girls of the night
I send two letters to them at home and get back none

My shawl and new bonnet are taken and burned
'A girl of ill fame' are the words used to slight
Windfalls hawked from a basket make a living for one

The gaslight in the prison hasn't the glow of the sun
The Gaoler brings a clergyman to show me the light
I send two letters to them at home and get back none

The gaol's terrible walls will keep me from ruin
I curse the oakum I'm picking by day and by night
Windfalls hawked from a basket make a living for one

I am now what I will always be, a girl of the night,
But red apples, green apples will start my new life,
I send two letters to them at home and get back none
Windfalls hawked from a basket make a living for one

IL-MARA RIEQDA
The Sleeping Lady, Malta

I have slept
sideways on a plinth
for three thousand years,
my pleated skirt
over the whale of my hip,
ankle-long, for modesty.

In my oracular dreams
I am made ugly, thin,
my plump breasts
no bigger than the
shrunken paps
of a pupless bitch.

But, thank the Deities,
these are only nightmares,
my pudginess remains,
and – it's whispered –
my roly-poly form
is *very* twenty-first century.

VENUS IN A BOTTLE

Legless but harmless,
stretched on the Métro platform,
bottle in her hand.

QUENELLES

Laid out before us
are our quenelles.

Their name suggests
a slaking draught,

notes dropped from
a reedy whistle,

the whomp of wings
through thin air,

carriages screeking
on a lofty railway,

an altered 'When?'
with twinned girls,

a pair of killing blades,
curved, whetted, waiting.

But they are none
of those things,

these delicate dumplings
of sweet river-pike;

pounded, piped and poached,
they steam before us,

reclaiming their name
with the first bite.

PANDEMIC

Fun-size women
bite each others' backs,
every flesh-inch
tasted and tested
against their own

They pay lip service
to mealtimes where
each swallowed
and supped morsel
is scaled, good or bad

In their seeded, split
wine-apple cores
they want to be
small above all else:
little girl as alien species

STRETCH

There's a stretch of time
reaching behind that's
as taut as a length of cat-gut,
it threads right through you,
stitched as snug as the baby
who made a drum of your belly,
it holds you to that moment.

There's a knot in the line,
no pulling hand over hand
can un-kink to drag you to here,
you'll stay where we left you,
under the late December sky,
that oozed white light
like cut, raw potato.

MANEEN
for Finn

When you eased into our world,
corded, with soft, boiled skin,
we welcomed you with laughter

Now, you malaprop your way through
the day, with 'sweels' for wheels,
'head-up' for hood, 'urse' for us

And our laughter still falls
at your soft robustness, your giddy heart,
your slender-fingered hair twirling

You who are one part of each of us
but so wholly yourself, a wonder child,
our golden maneen.

POSITIVE MANTRA, GIVEN TO ME IN A DREAM,
ON THE NIGHT OF THE DAY I RECEIVED YET ANOTHER
PUBLISHER'S REJECTION FOR MY FIRST NOVEL

Because I can
and because I can
and because I can
I will

RETICENT

That heart that
you have pinned
to your sleeve
is bleeding
onto my skin

Drip, drop, flood.

But I'm happy
to let it,
it's the only
way I have
to read you.

CELEBRATION DAYS

Bring me flowers, lover,
blossoms that will
match who I am:
weeping willows,
death-heavy orchids,
anything dolorous
or melancholic.

Make me a card
and write your
own words on it:
falsified verse can't
lift my sacred heart,
my blood is frozen red
like a plastic Jesus.

And pour two flutes
of pear-sweet,
piss-pale *prosecco*,
that we can clink
to ourselves,
me, the moody chatterer,
you, the eternal balmer.

I am made in
this awkward way,
sloughing off love's
graces like so many
unwanted skins,
yet, in my deep inside,
I am raw from neglect.

You celebrate me, lover,
by putting me back together,
gifting me to myself.

Acknowledgements

Thanks go to the editors of the following publications in which many of these poems first appeared: *Poetry Ireland Review, The SHOp, Crannóg, Black Mountain Review, Hiberno-English Archive, The Stony Thursday Book, Burning Bush,* Arlen House's *!DIVAS! A Sense of Place* anthology, *west 47, ROPES, River King Supplement, Niederngasse, deaddrunkdublin, Electric Acorn, The Red Wheelbarrow, Garm Lu* and the US anthology *Generation X: In Our Own Words.*

The poem *Our Lady of Dublin* was shortlisted for the Hiberno-English Poetry Award. The poems *Tattoo, Stretch, Frida Kahlo's Palette, Through the Deep, Like Dogs to War, Pink Lungs* and *Quarry Men, Dublin, 1868* were collectively shortlisted for the Firewords Poetry Prize.

For support, friendship and love, special thanks go to Alan Hayes, John Dillon, Órfhlaith Foyle, Finbar McLoughlin, Pat Jourdan, Joyce Little and all the O'Connors. Thanks to Marcus Hughes for the wonderful cover image. And big thanks to my darling sons, Cúán and Finn, for being themselves.